Butterflies and Birds

Nature Coloring Book

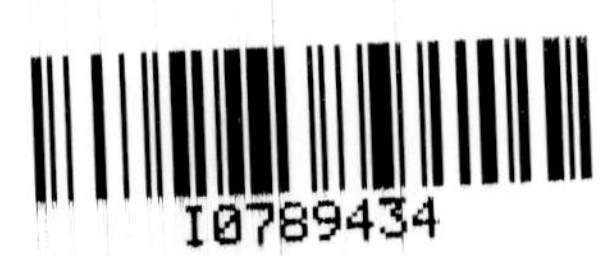

ISBN-13:978-1976019784

ISBN-10:1976019788

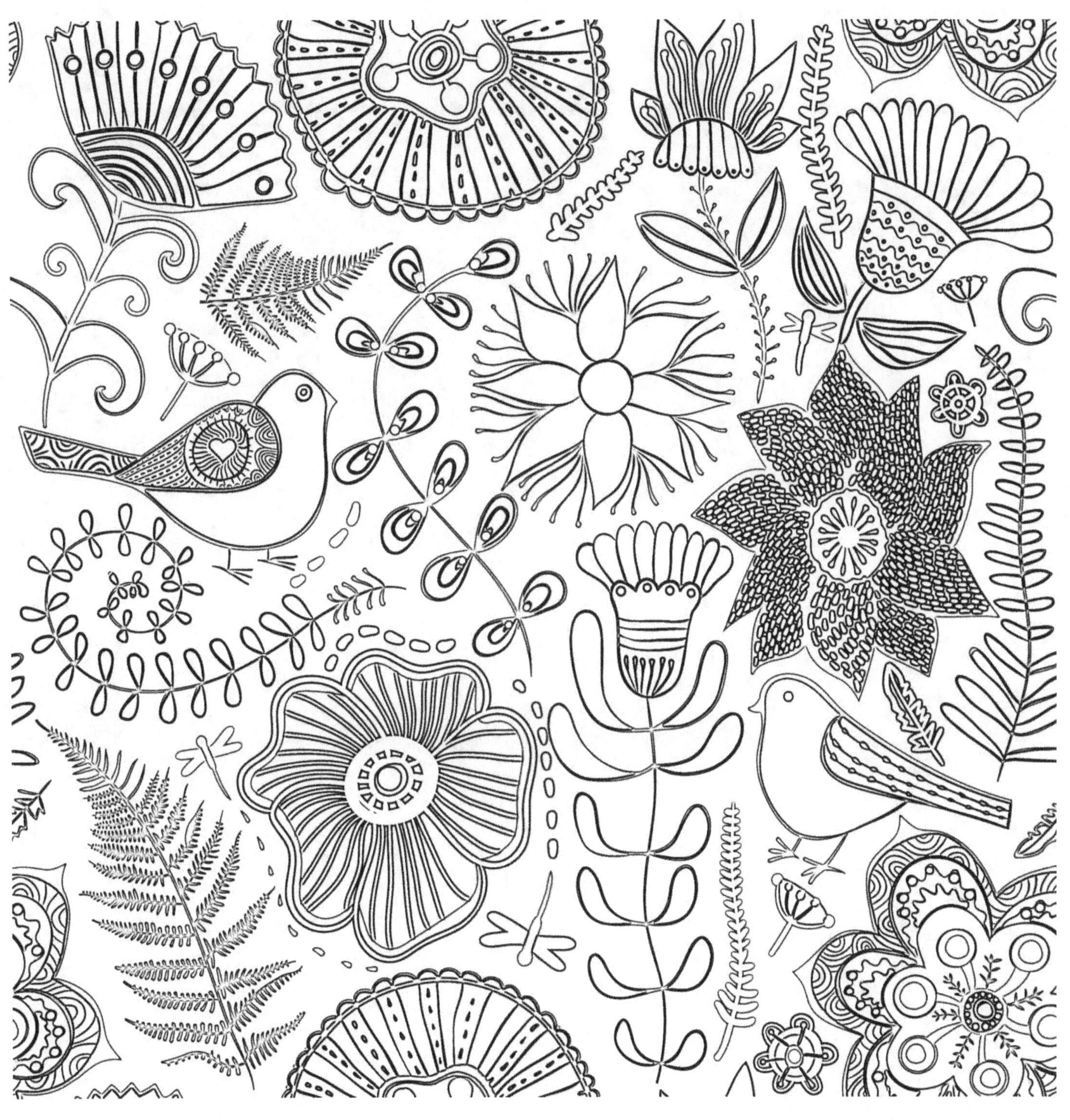

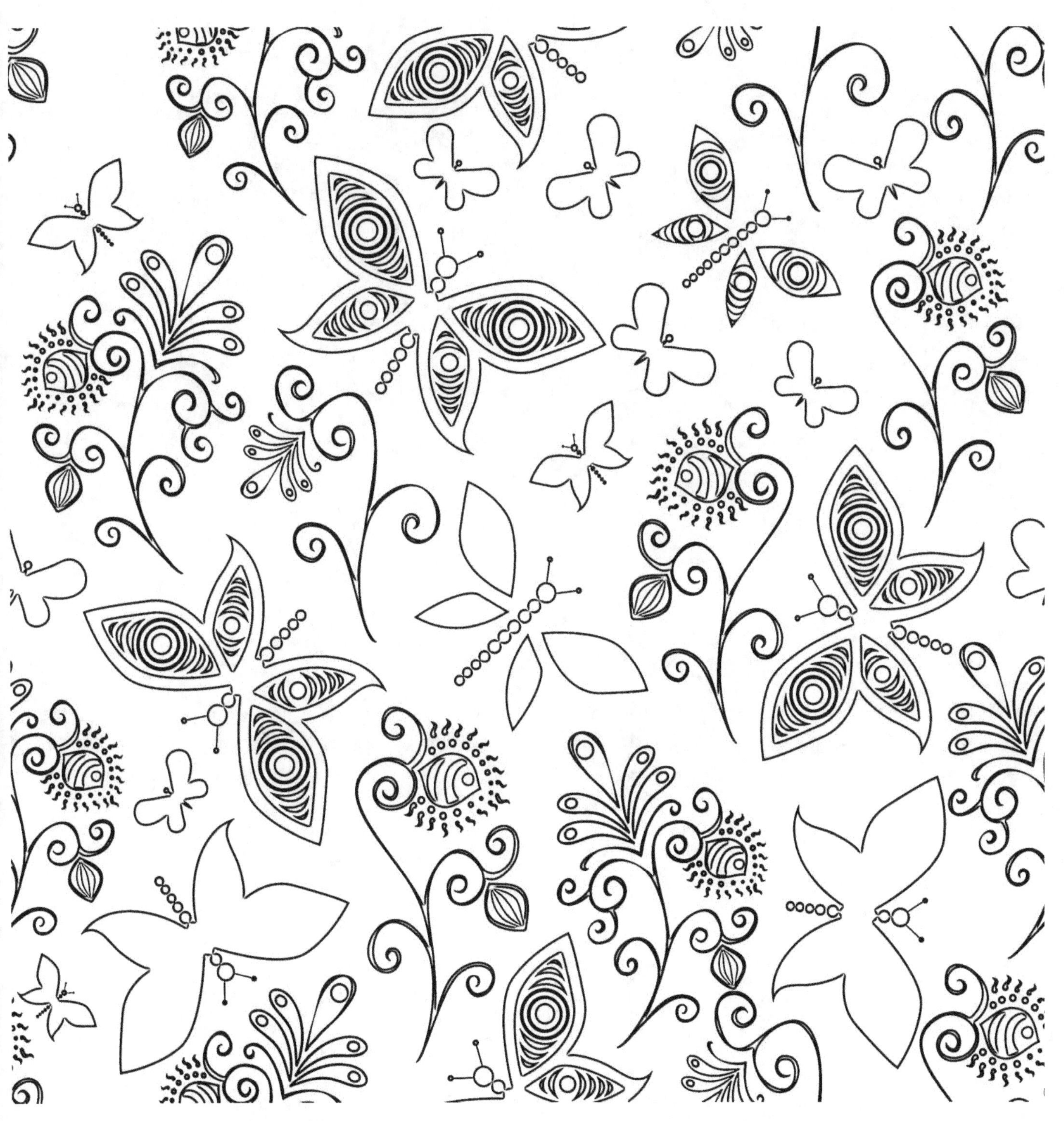

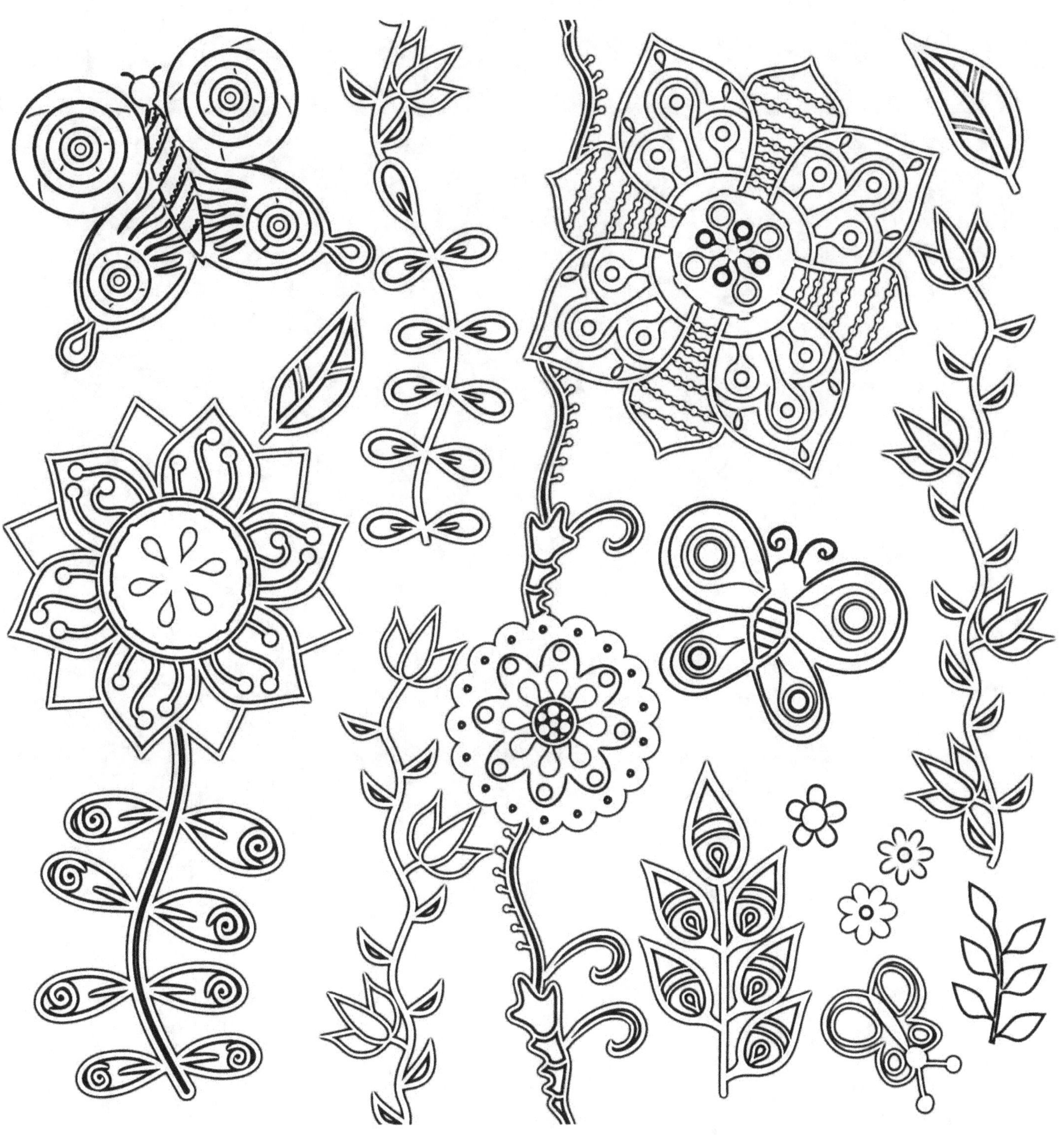

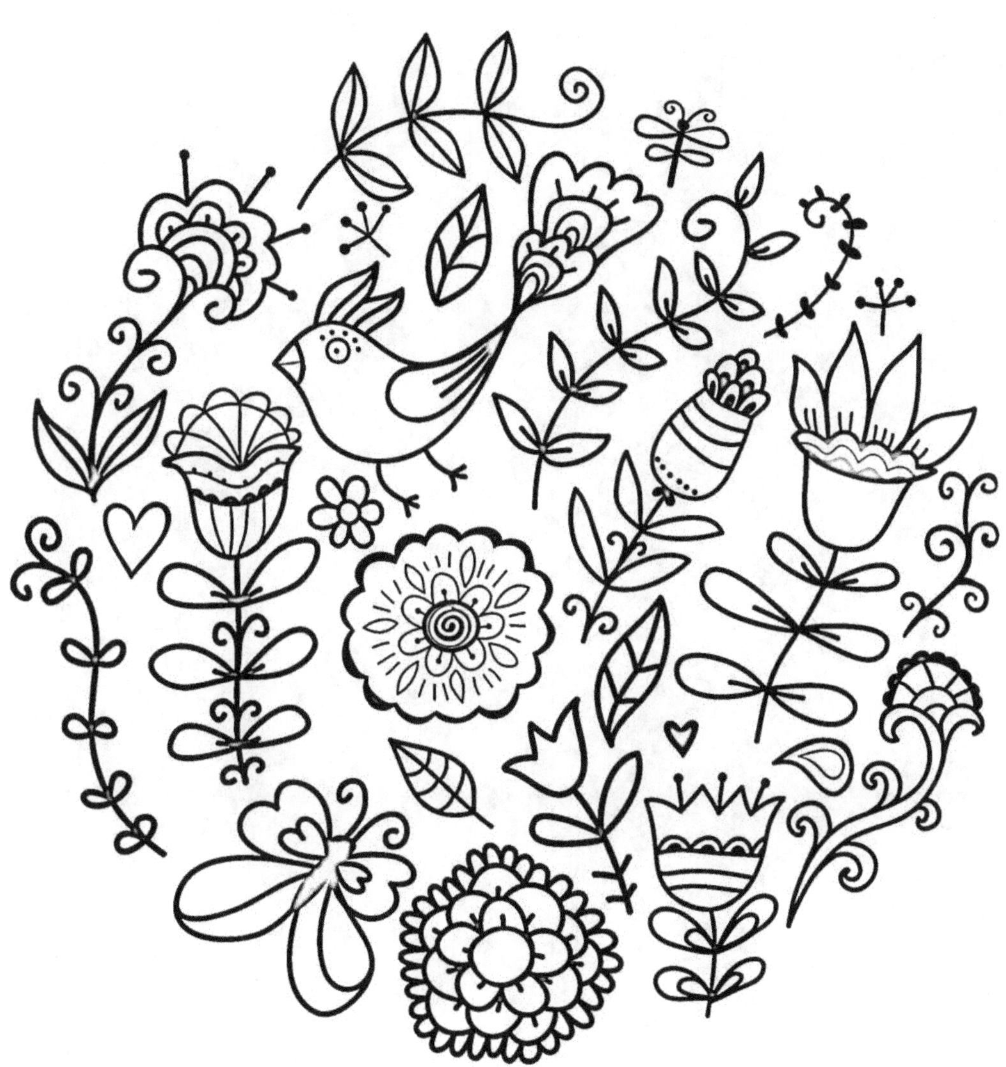

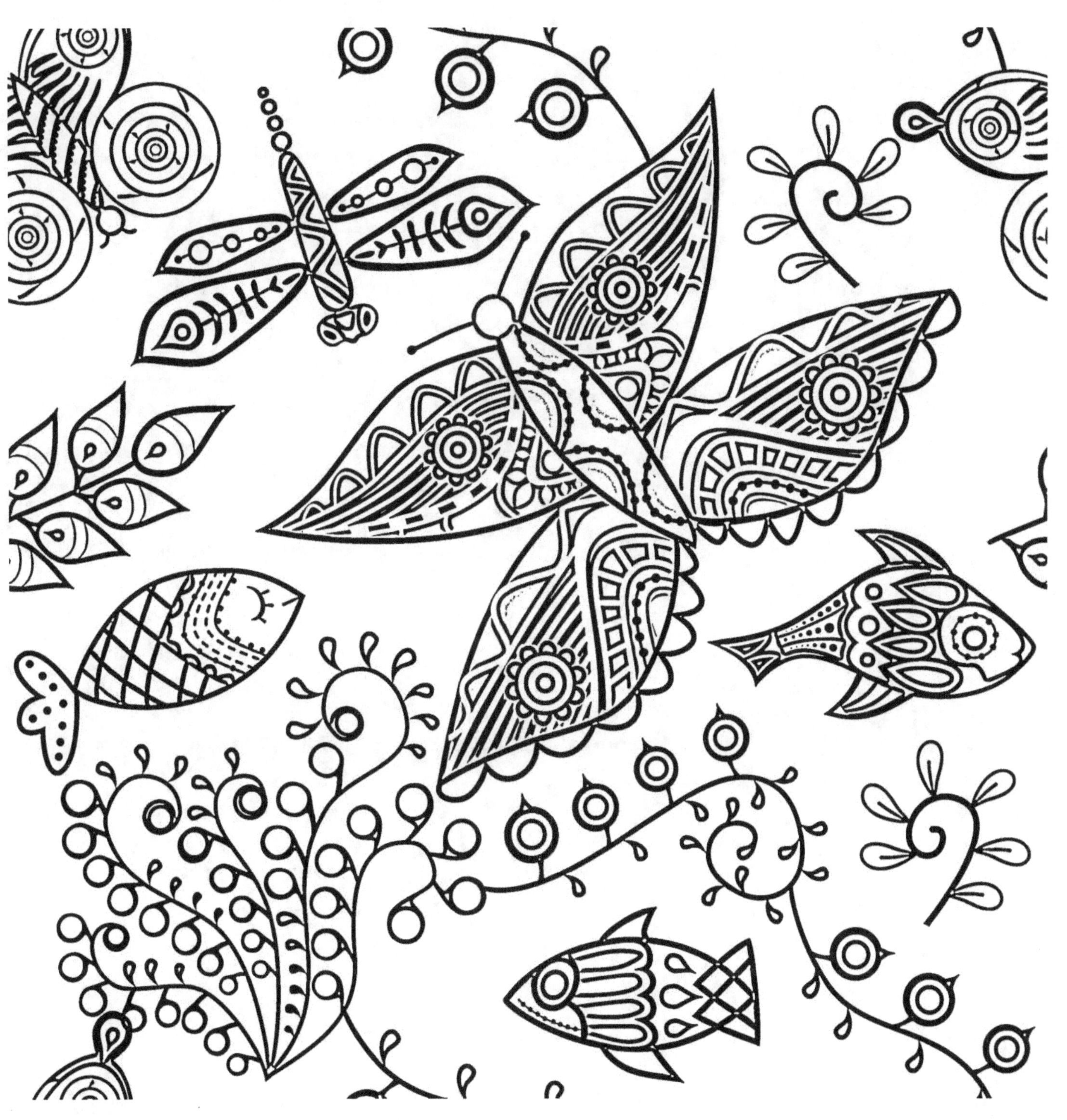

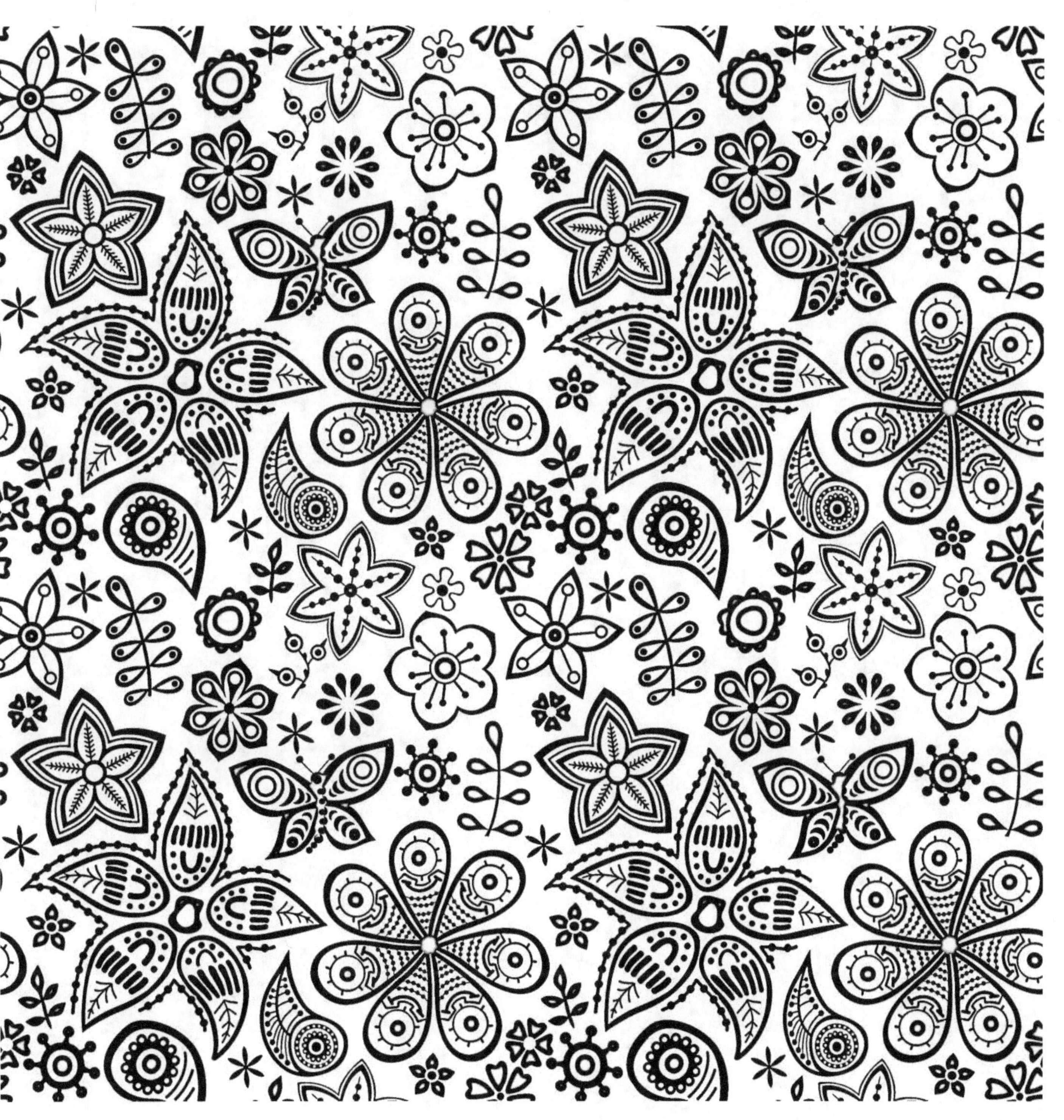

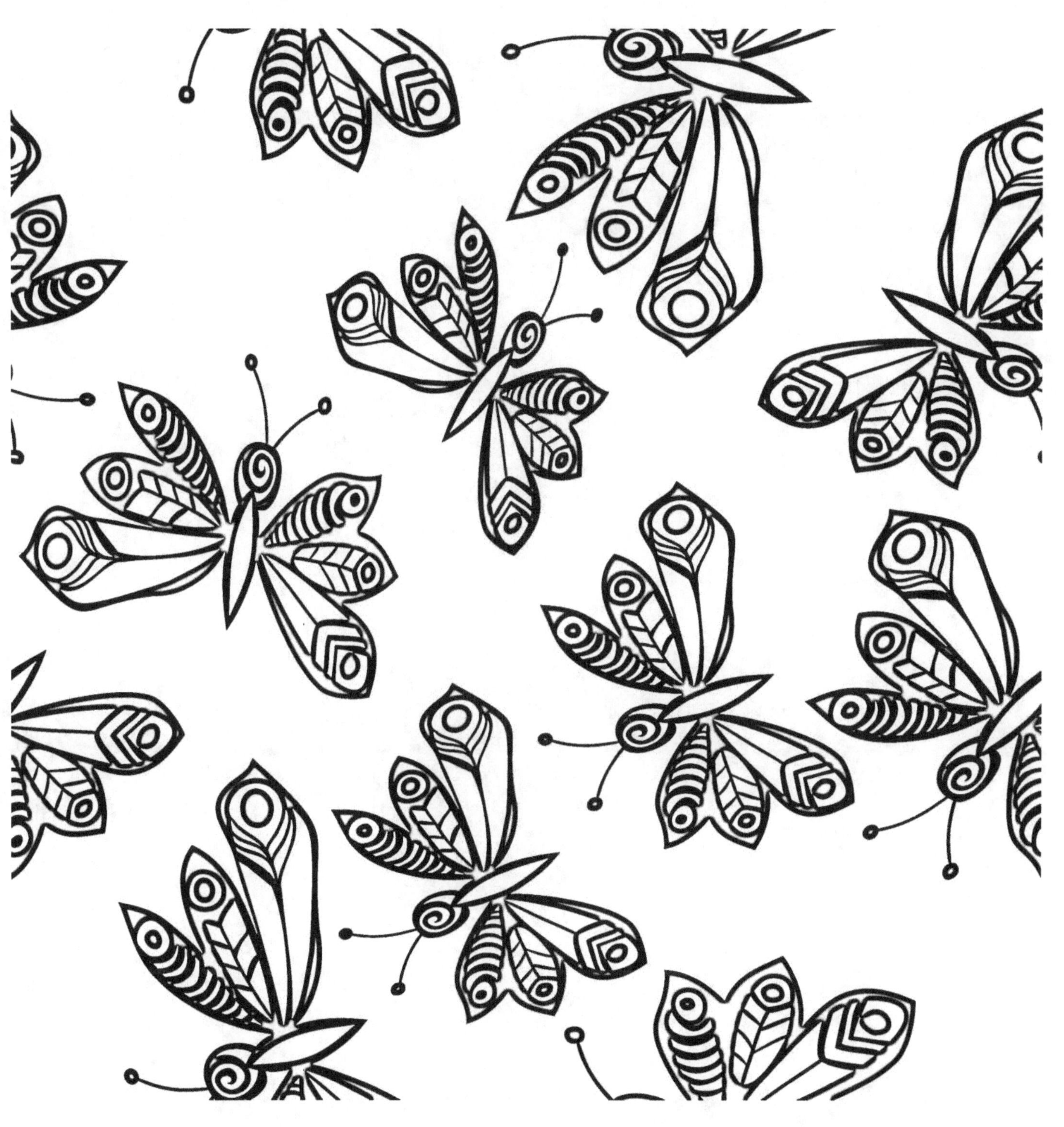

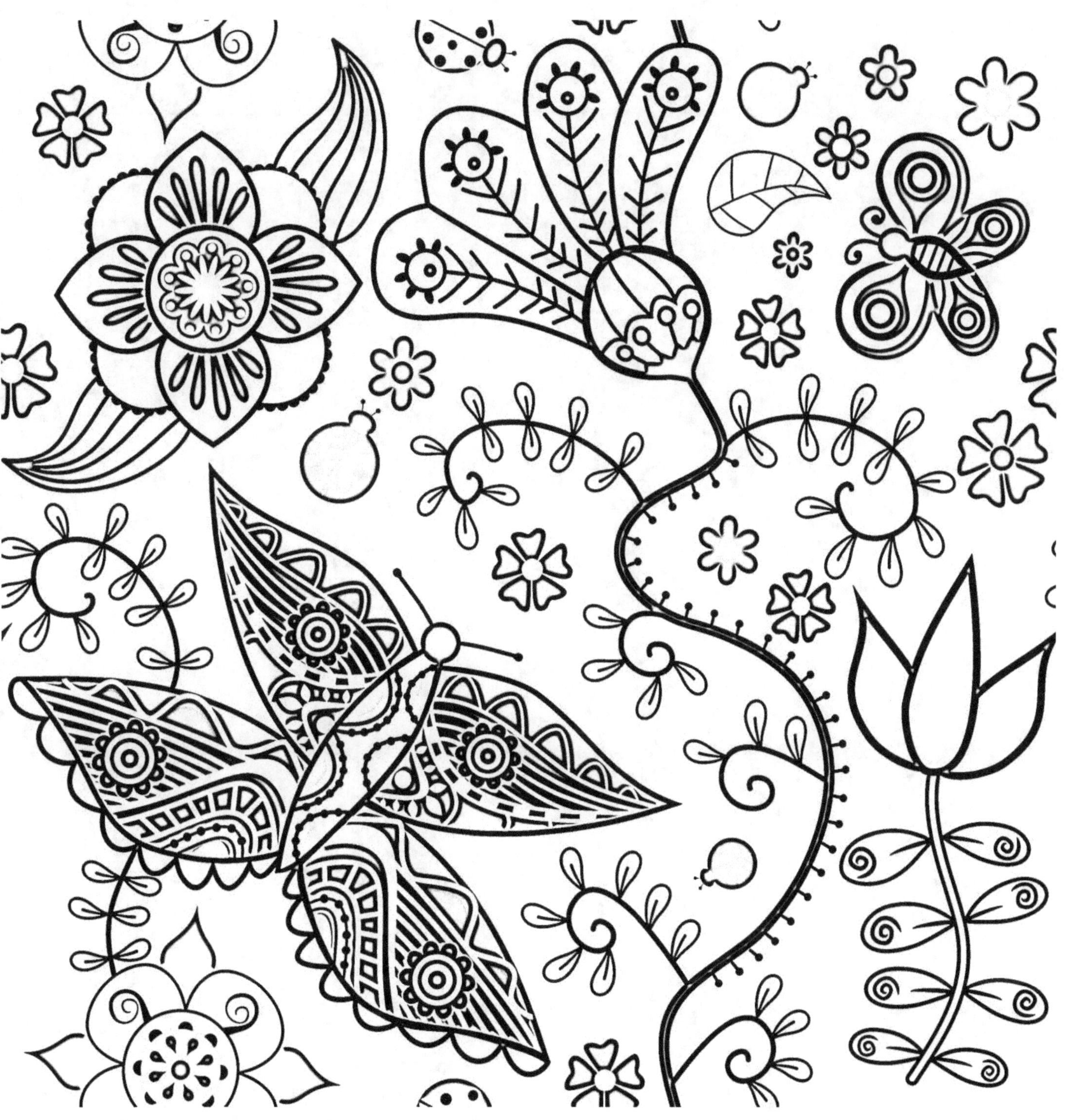

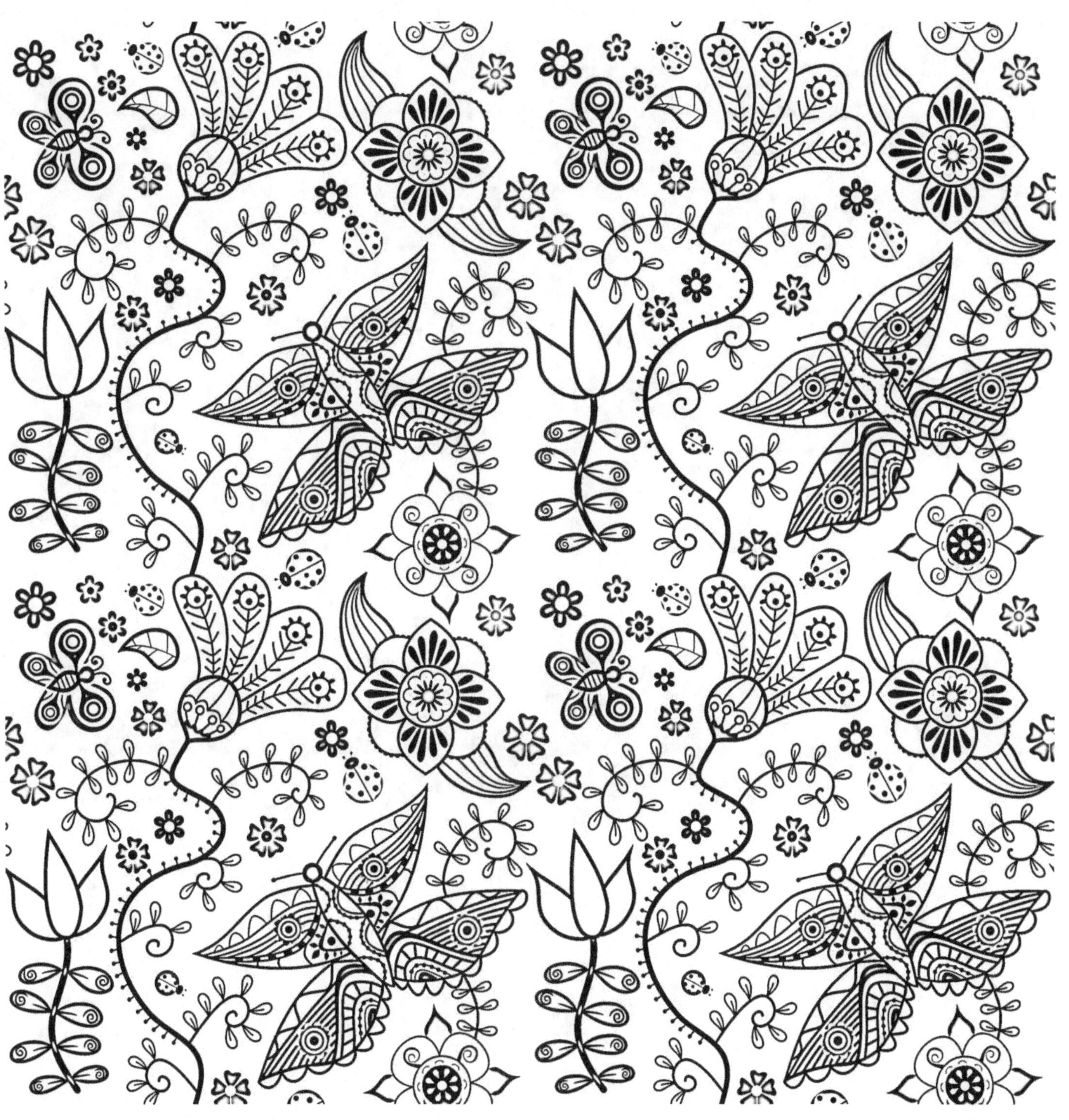

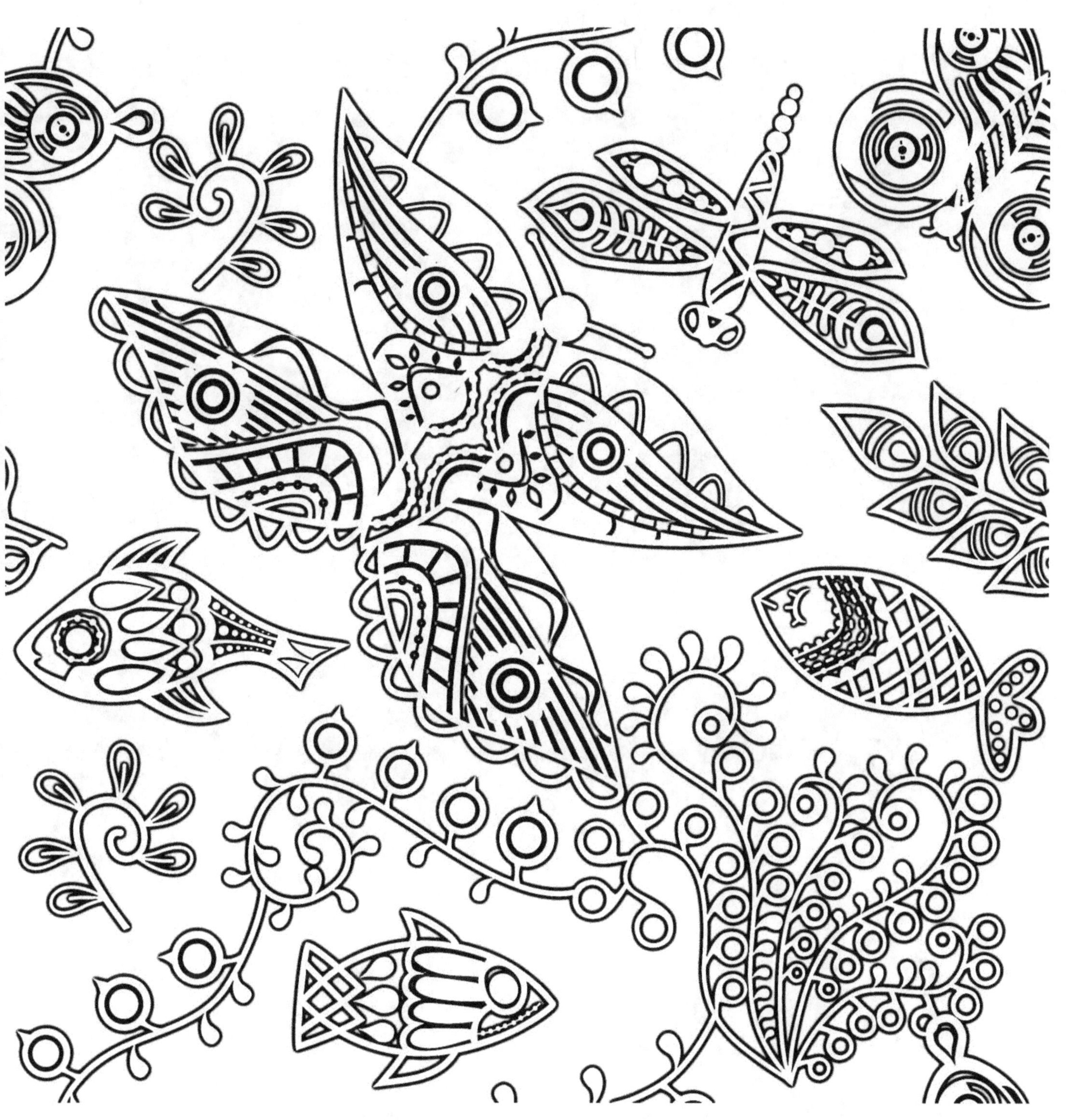

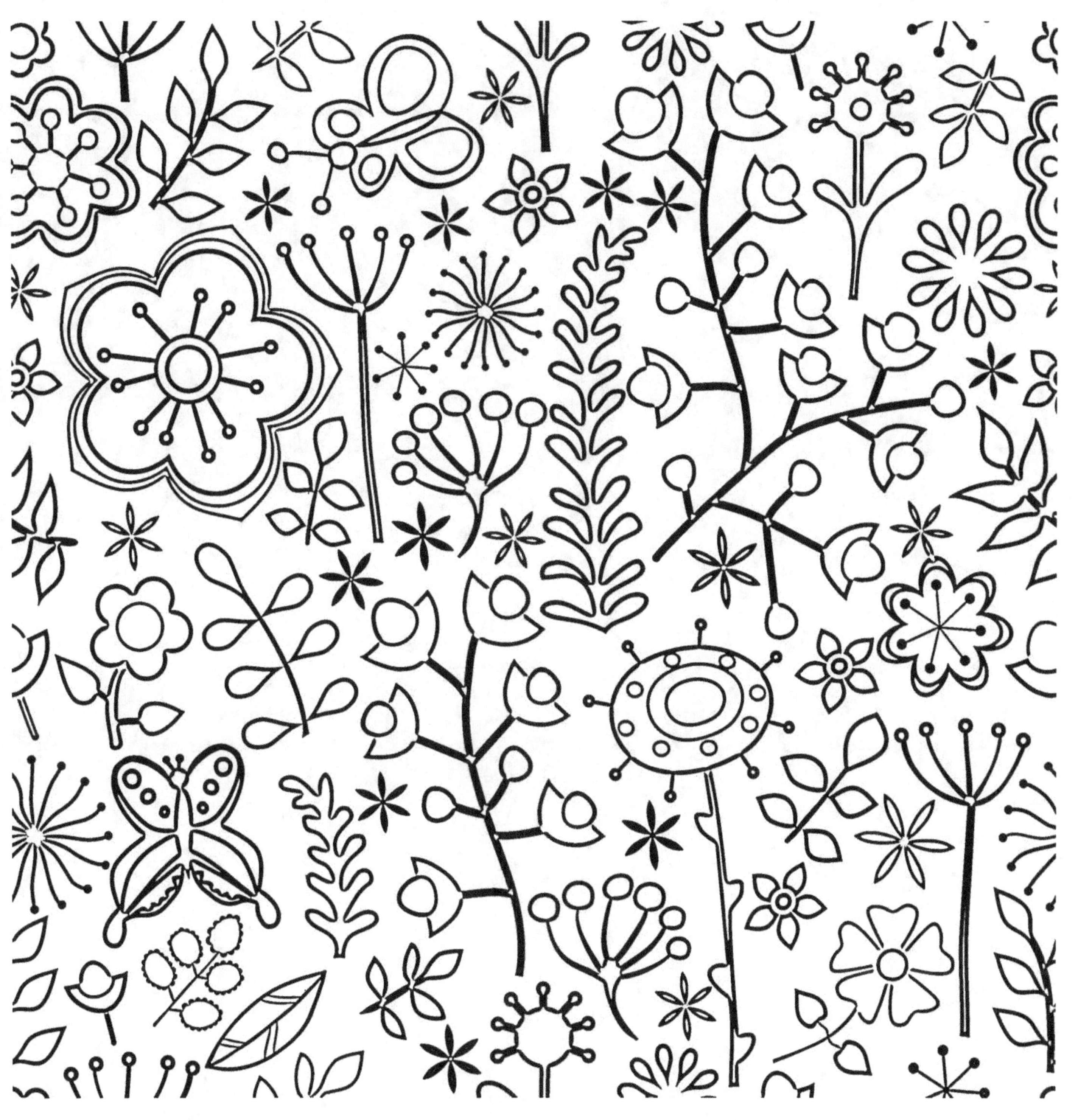

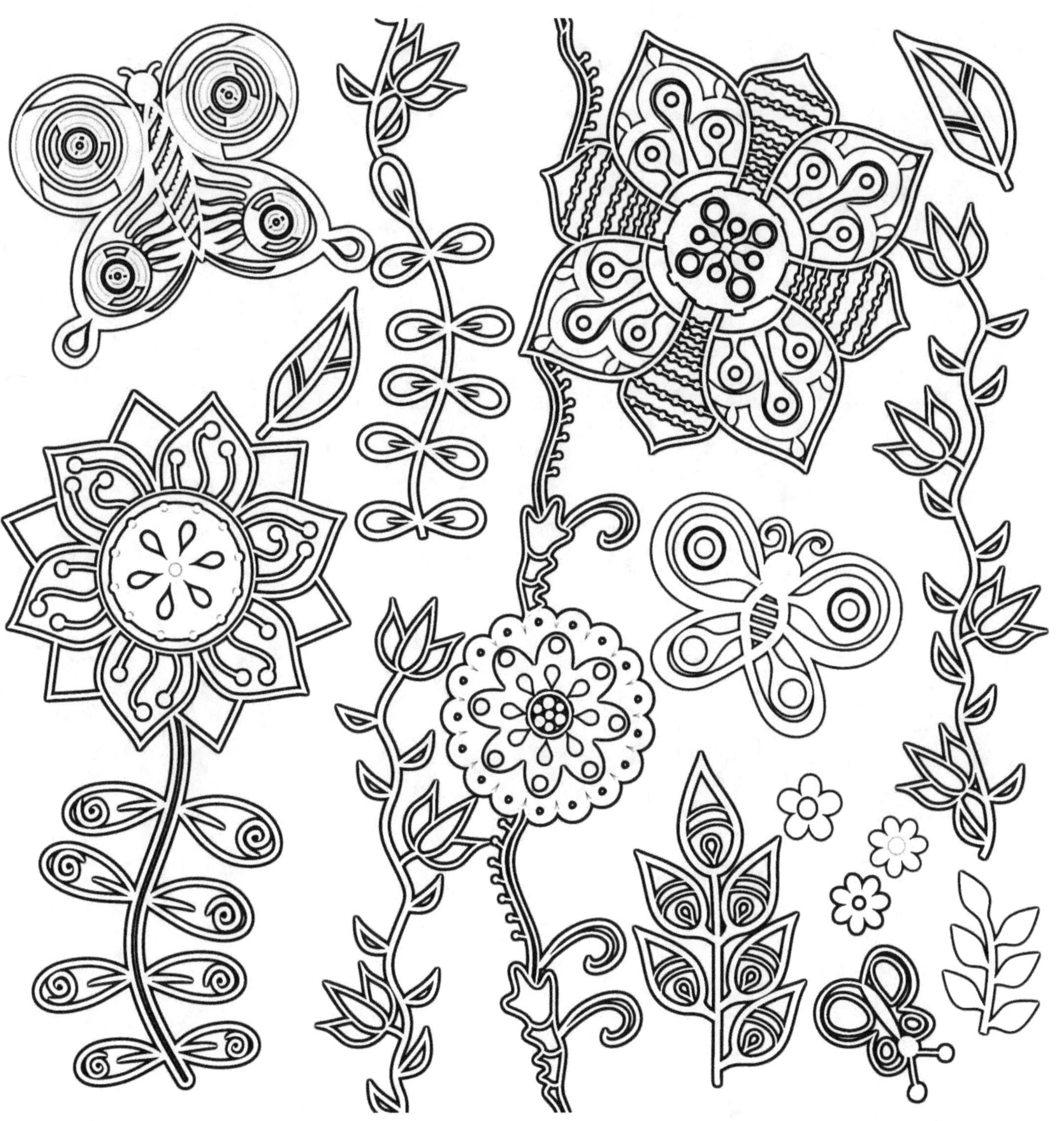

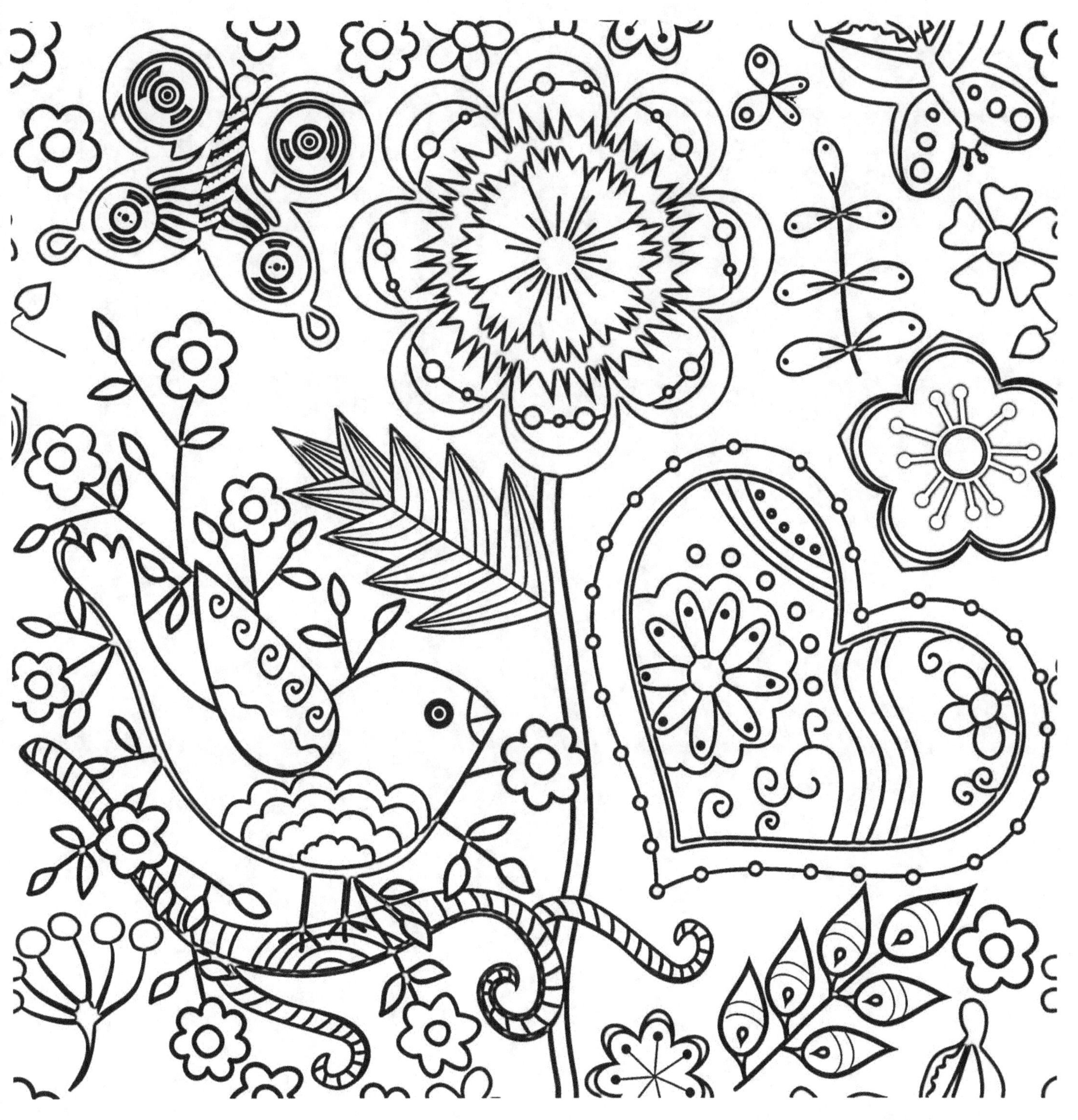

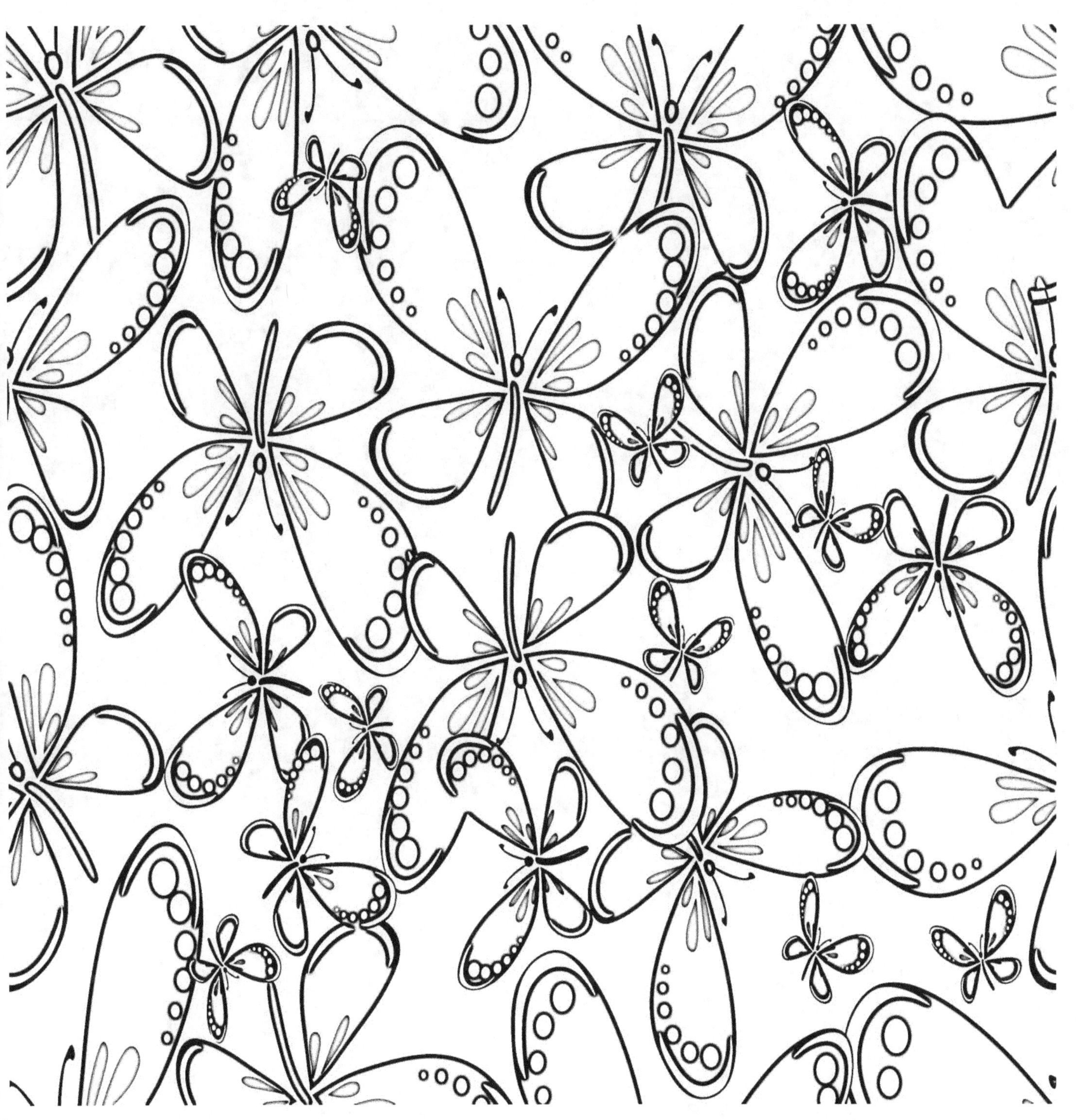

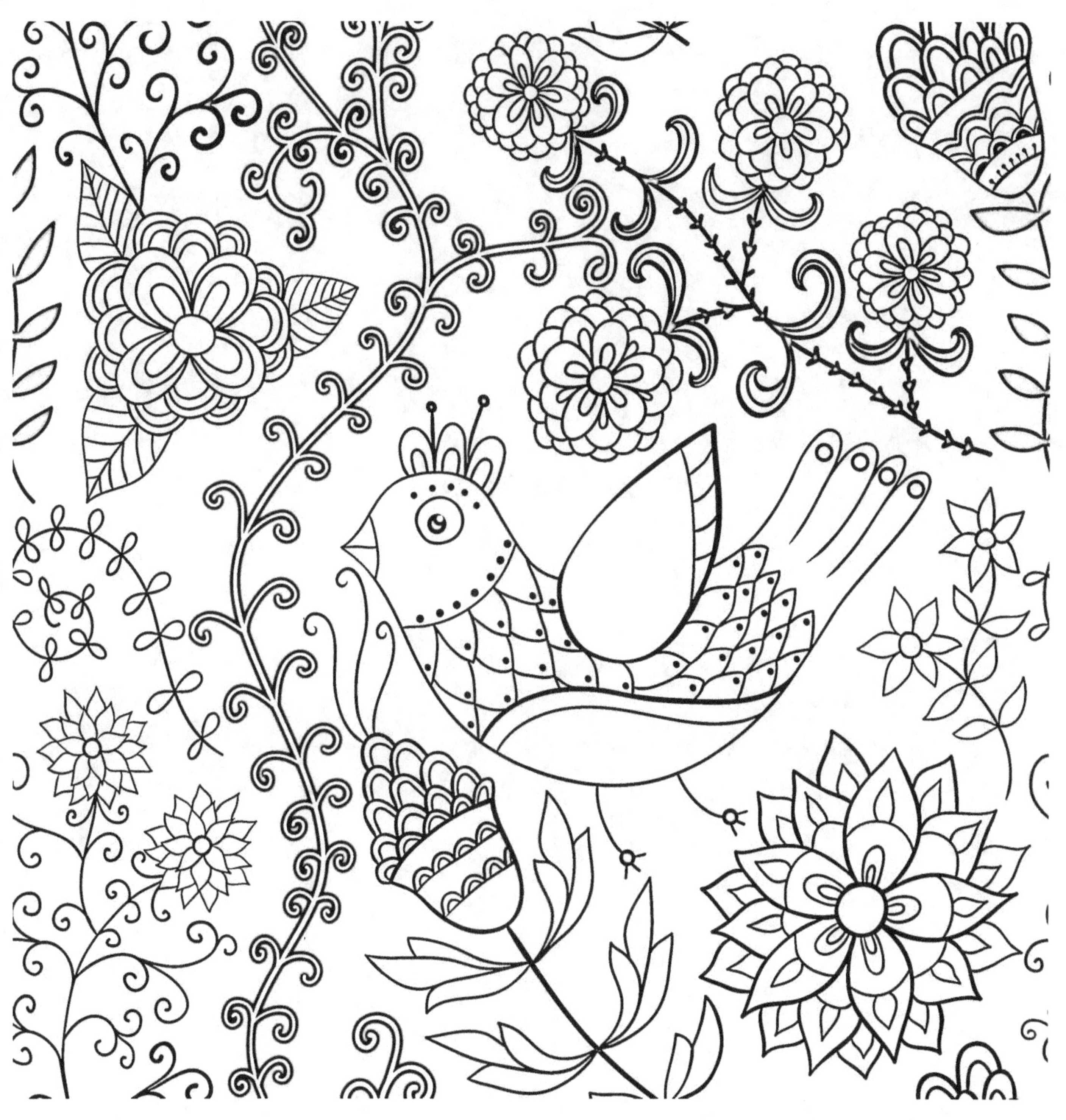

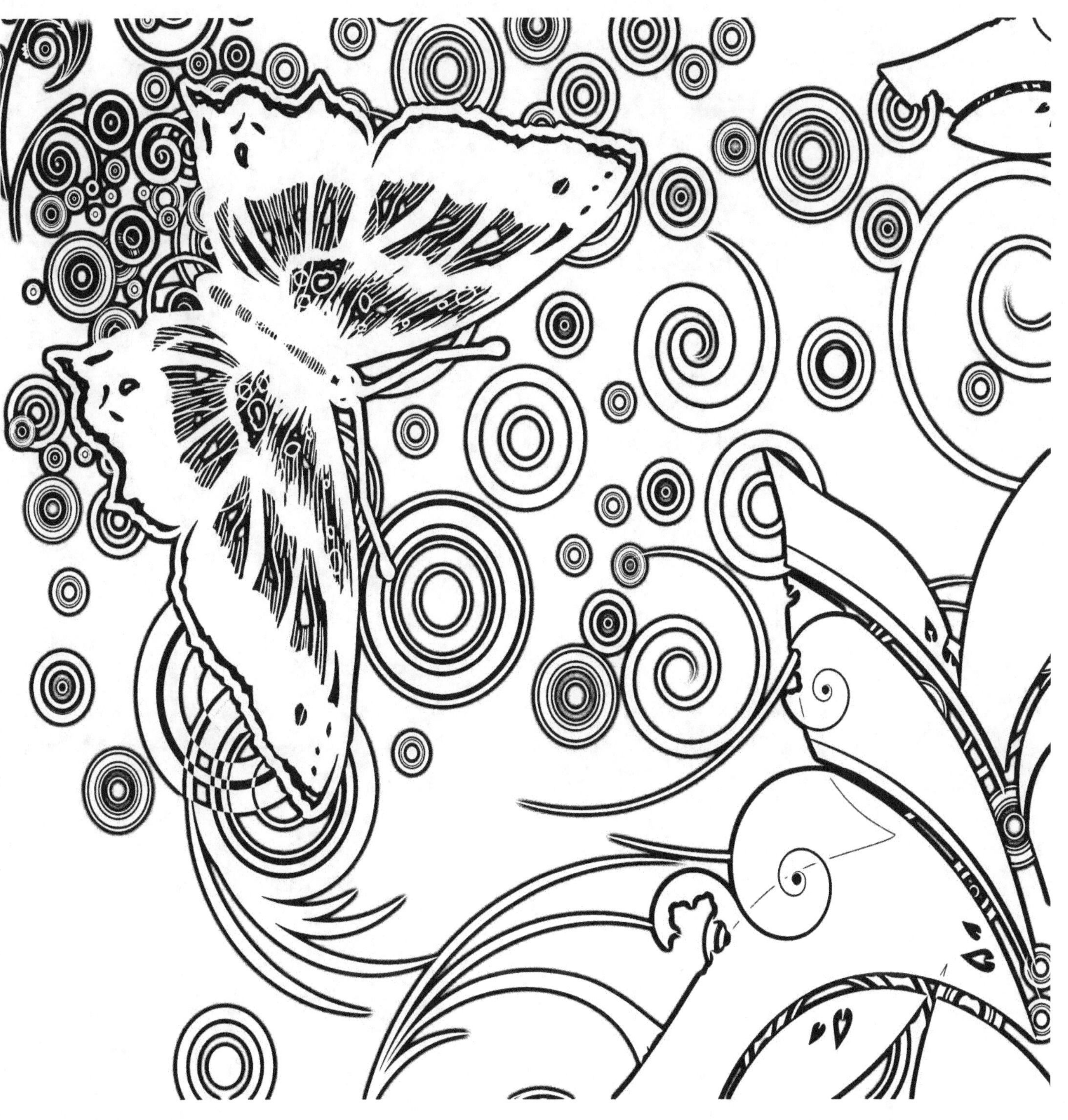

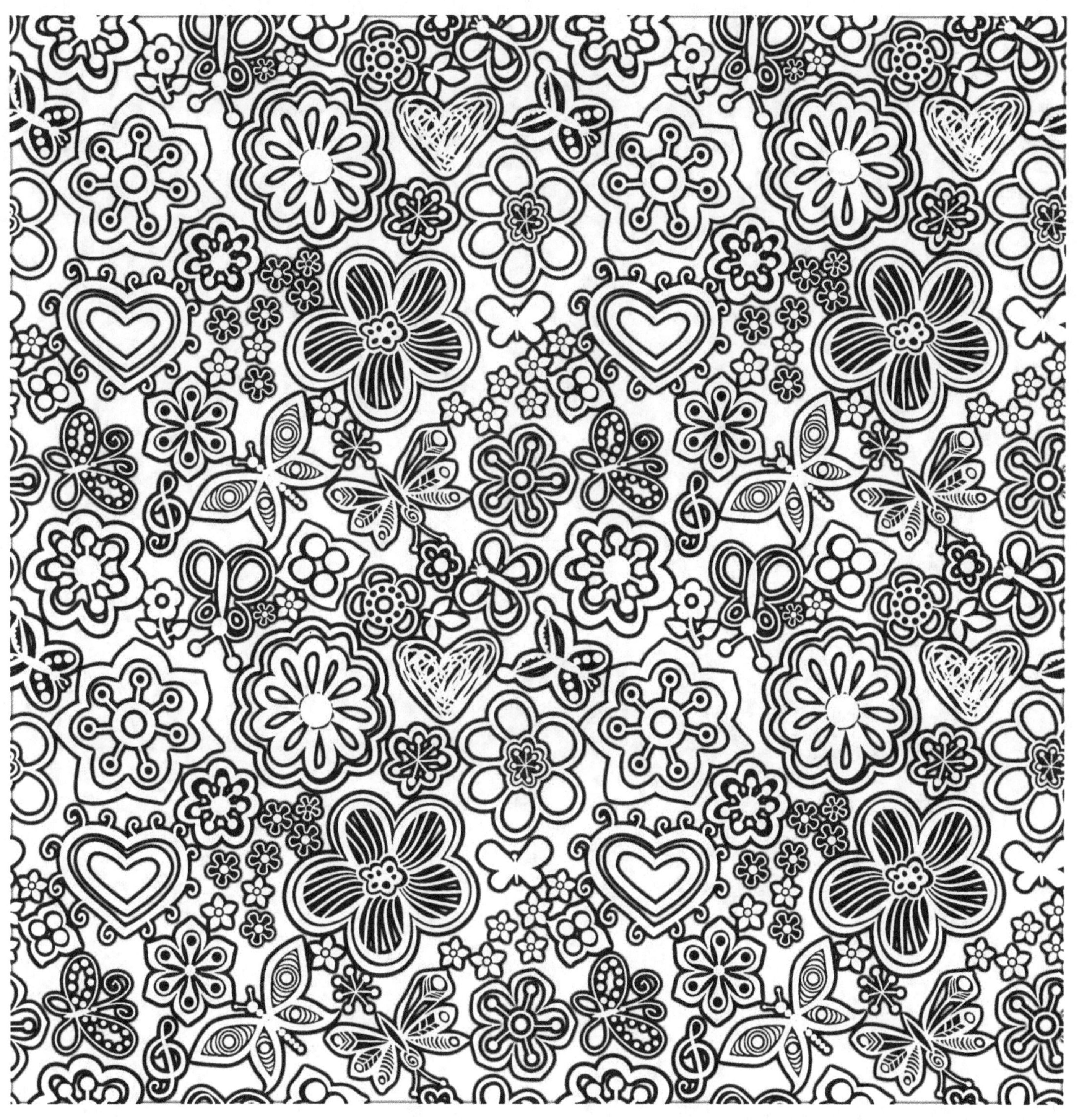

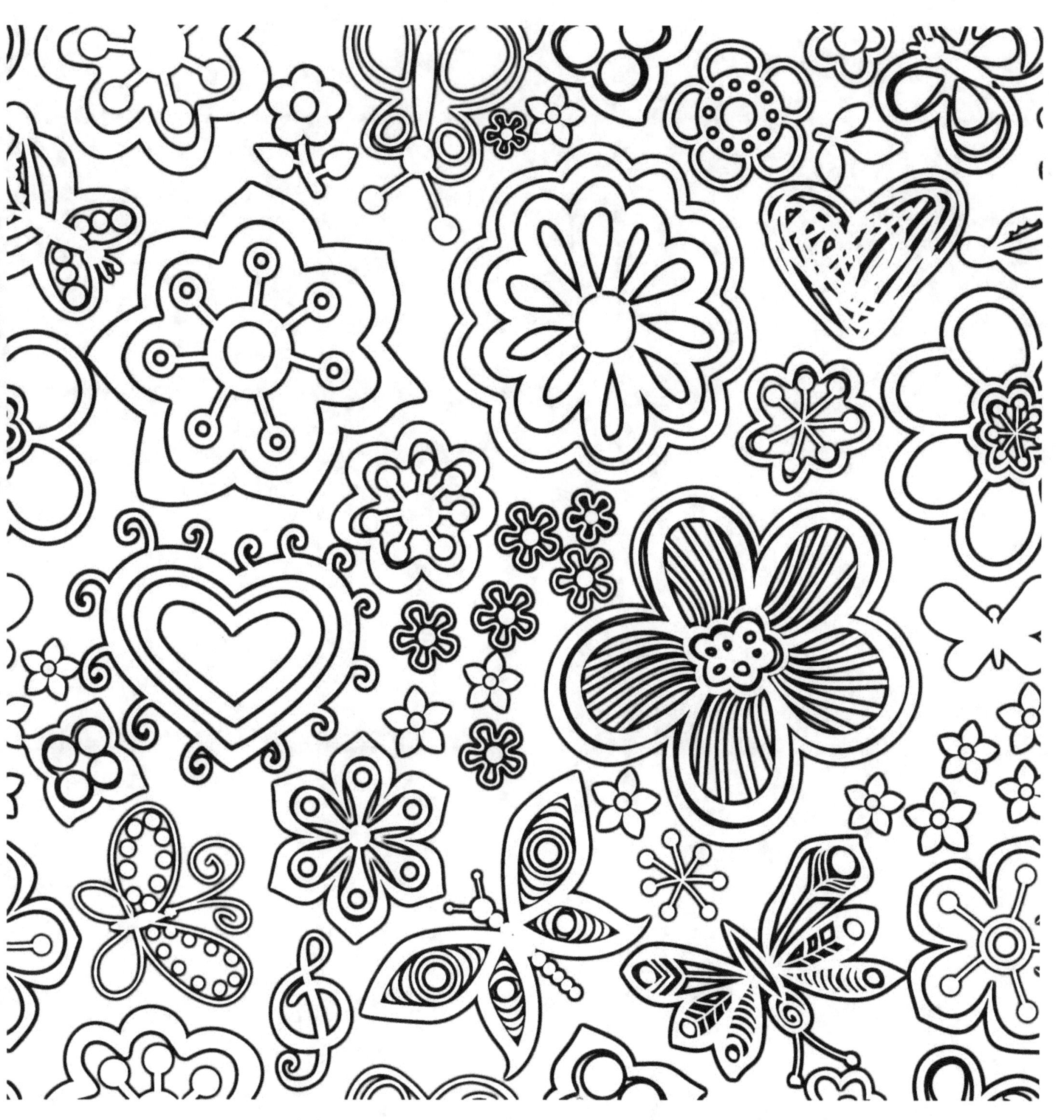

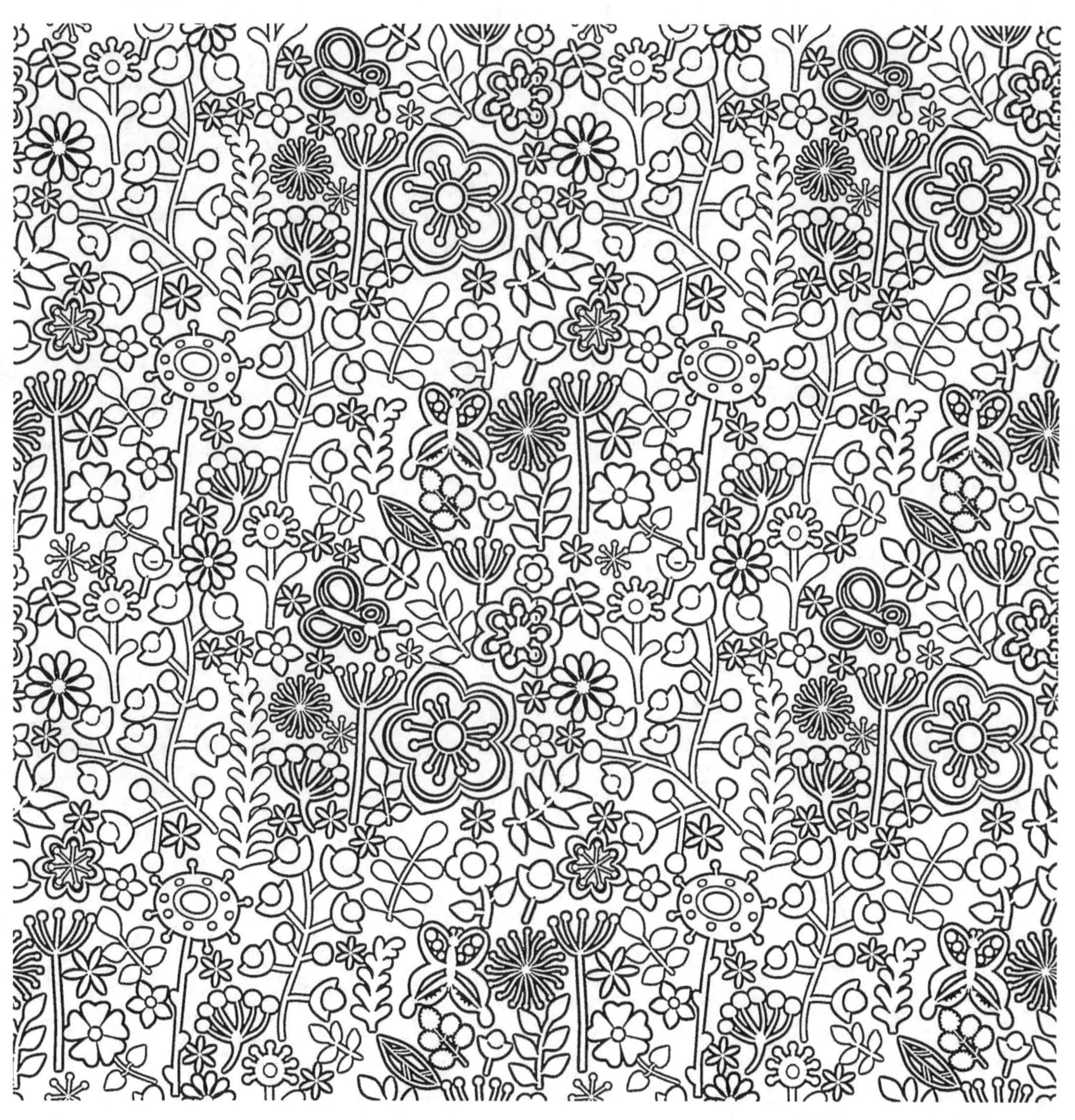

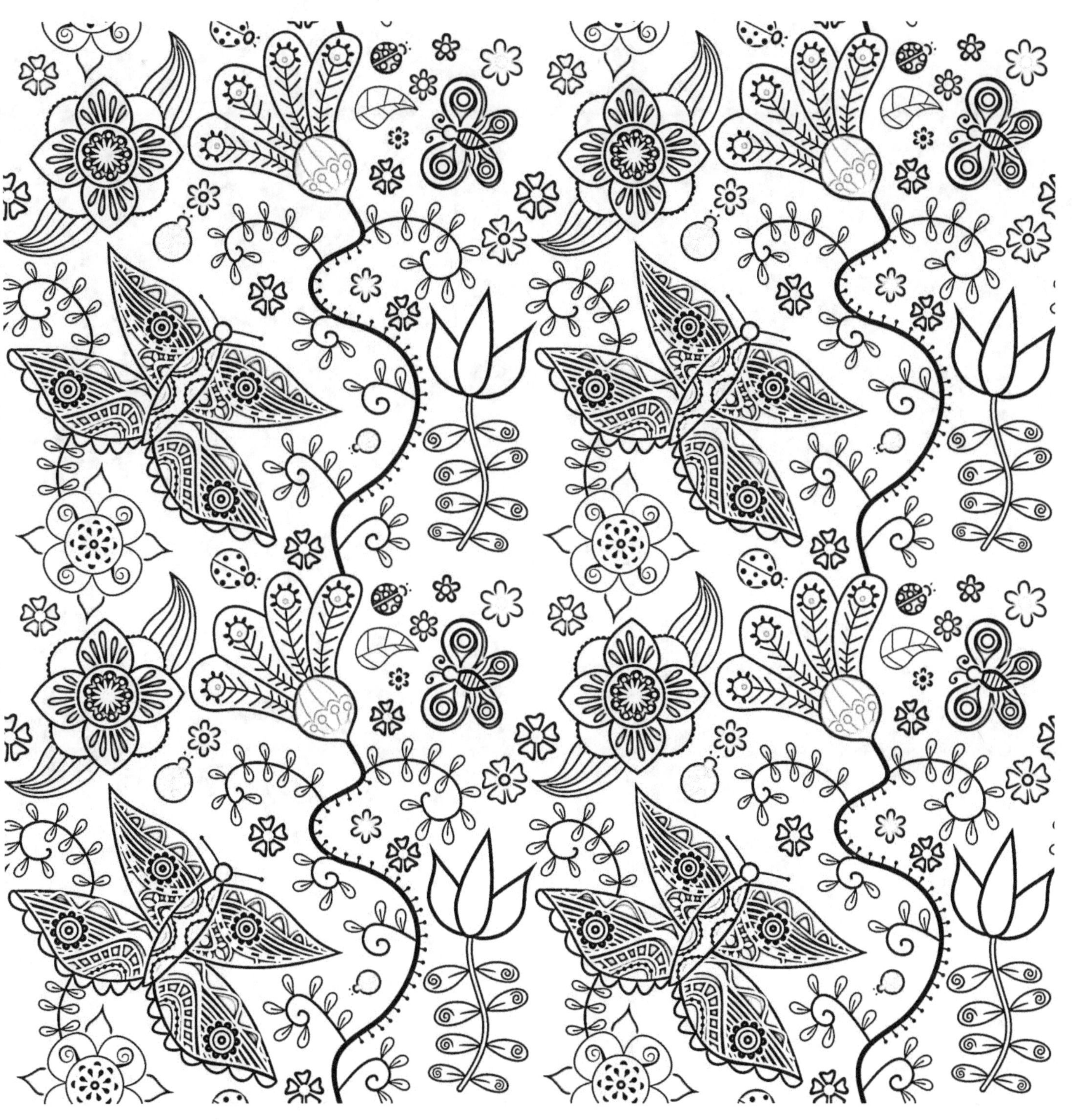

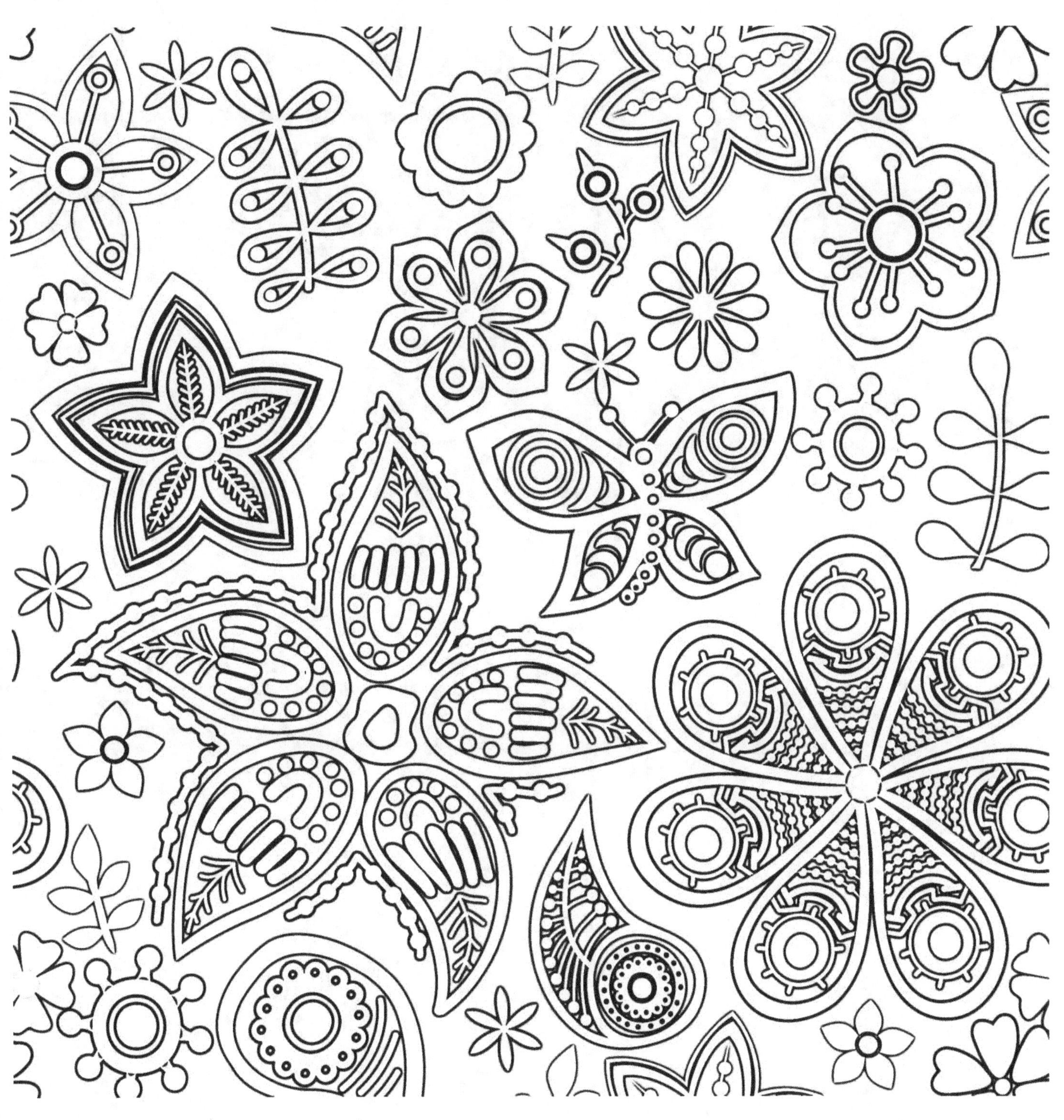

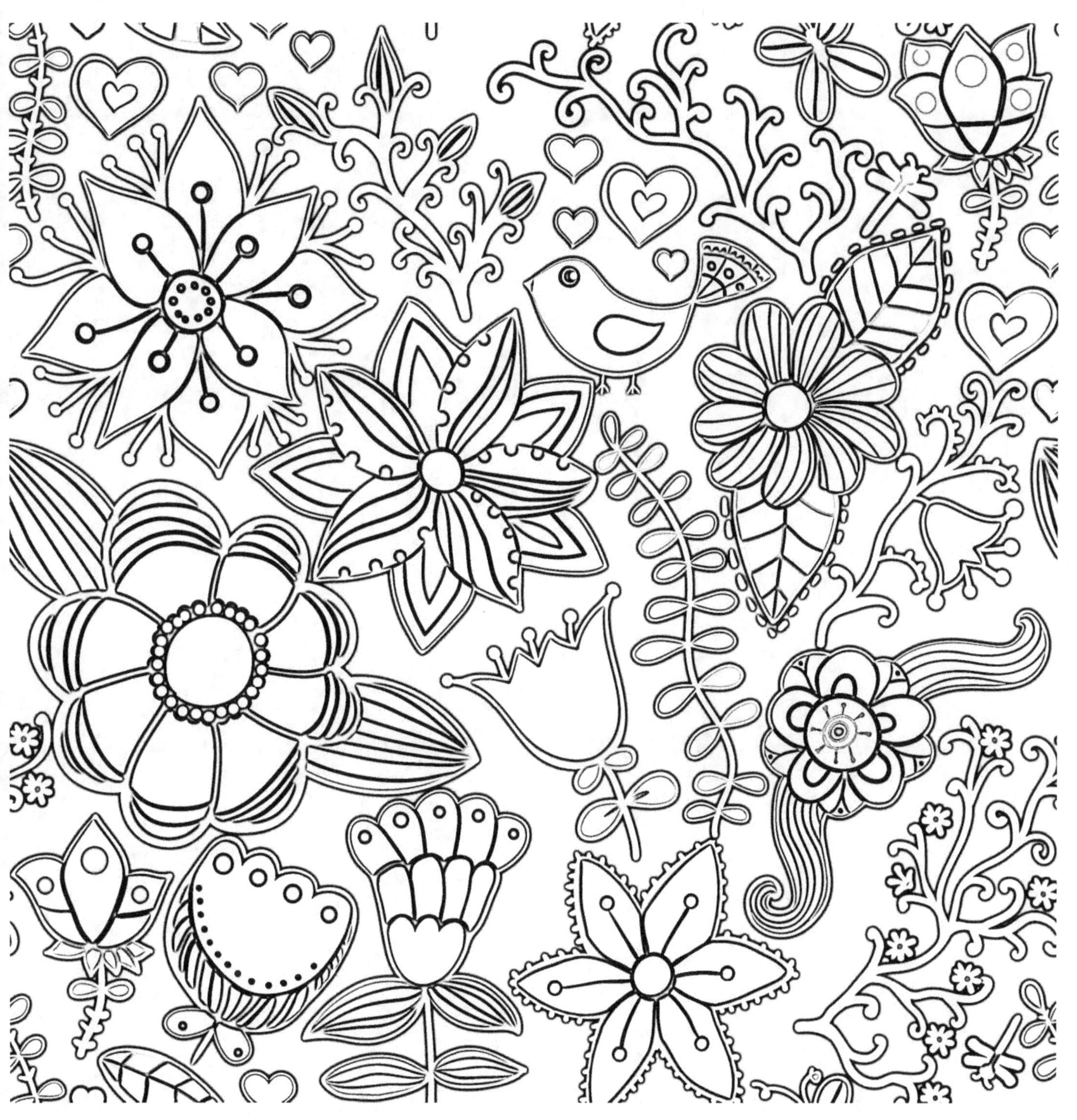

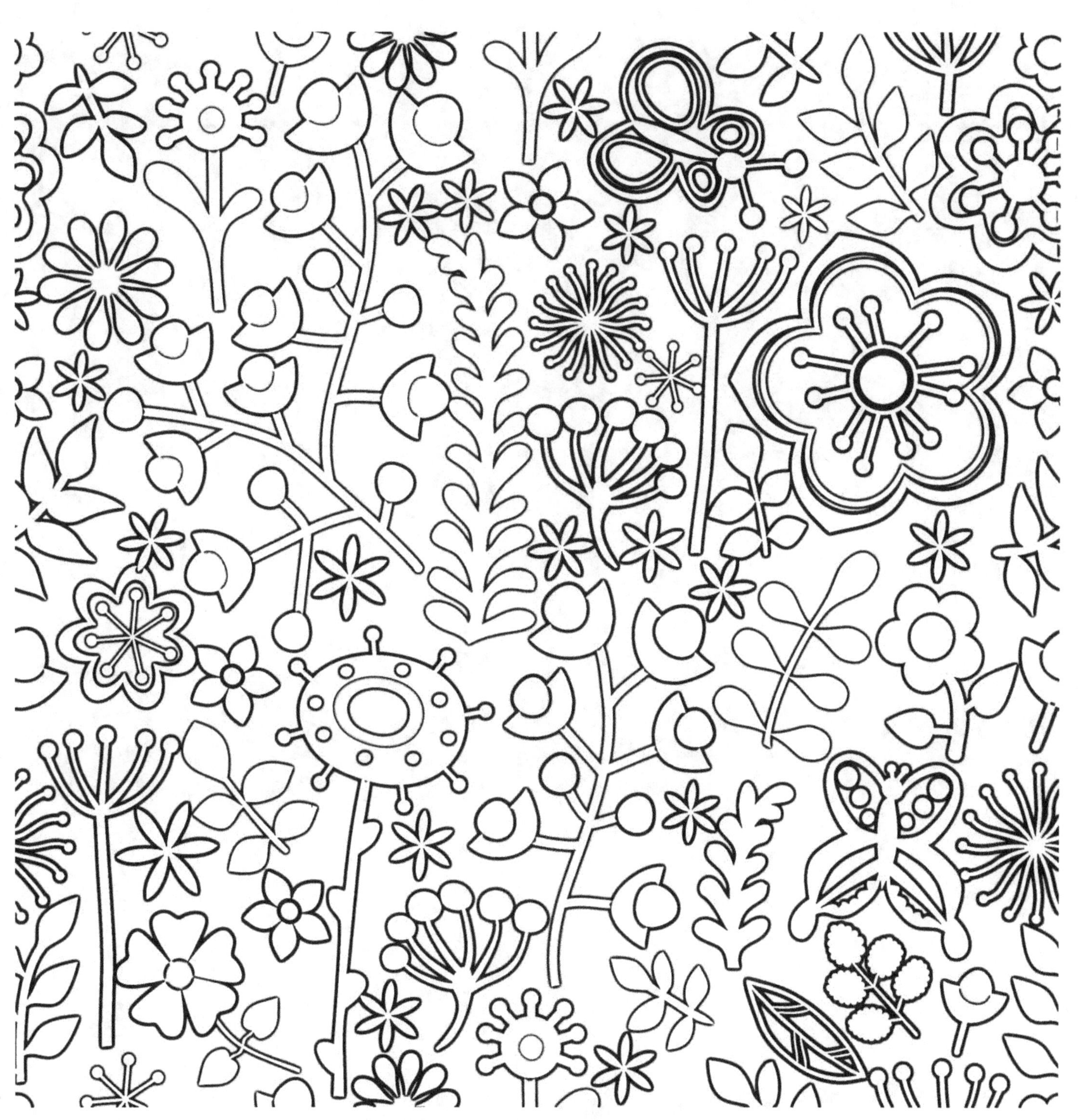